how happy is
your
Home?

50 Great Tips to Bring More Health,
Wealth and Joy into Your Home

Sophie Keller

How Happy Is Your Home?
ISBN-13: 978-0-373-89248-8
© 2011 by Sophie Keller

Author photograph by Sarah Corwin Photography
Illustrations by Serena Zanello

Library of Congress Cataloging-in-Publication Data
Keller, Sophie.
  How happy is your home? : 50 great tips to bring more health, wealth, and joy into your home / Sophie Keller.
        p. cm.
Includes bibliographical references.
ISBN 978-0-373-89248-8 (hardback)
1. Home economics—Philosophy. 2. Well-being. 3. Feng shui in interior decoration. I. Title.
TX13.K45 2011
640--dc22
                    2011010359

How Happy Is is a trademark of Sophie Keller.

www.Harlequin.com

Printed in U.S.A.

To Oli and Judah. Home is where my heart is

CONTENTS

INTRODUCTION

Feng shui (pronounced "Fung shway") means "wind and water." They are the two natural elements that move and flow on the earth and are the basis for our survival—the air we breathe and the water we drink. The goal of feng shui is to help you maximize the beneficial movement and flow of chi (which is another word for "life force" or "energy") through your living space.

Whether you are in your home or not, the energy of your home environment has the ability to lift or drain your spirits throughout the day. It is thought that if the flow of chi in your home is strong, it will support all your endeavors in and out of the home. Similarly, if it is weak, it will pull you down.

You don't want the chi to move too fast and create anxiety or to move too slow and cause you to remain stagnant. You want it to enter easily in through your front door and move smoothly, like a calm breeze or gently flowing water, around every room in the house.

Feng shui is like acupuncture for your home. With the use of needles, acupuncture is known to release any blockages in the flow of chi throughout the body in order to create a steady movement of energy to all areas, keeping you vitalized, healthy and full of life. Feng shui works in much the same way. Your house is similar to a second body, as it is where you spend most of your time and is an expression of who you are. The "cures" that you are going to use from the feng shui toolbox are like the needles in acupuncture—they will help you release energy in your home in order for it to flow freely and for you to create a comfortable, relaxing and productive living space.

I was first introduced to feng shui in my late teens, but I took it seriously only later on, during a period when my life felt like it was falling apart. At the time I lost a job, my parents were both diagnosed with cancer, I split up with my boyfriend of three years and was suffering from an immune illness myself. To say it was a particularly trying time would be an understatement.

However, I tend to reach for a lifeline at moments in crisis and decided to throw myself into intense training to become a qualified practitioner of feng shui. As I made changes to my own home with feng shui, my life started to transform very quickly for the better, and my initial "prove it to me" attitude and skepticism were blown to pieces as I soon realized from personal experience how powerful this practice could actually be.

Since 2001 I have had the pleasure of helping hundreds of people by feng shui-ing their houses, offices and shops. Even as I started to write this book, a television writer came into my office and said, "Hey, Sophie. Do you remember me? You feng shuied my house seven years ago. I just wanted to tell you that a few months after you came to my home, I met my wife."

That same day I got a call from a client whom I had told to put flowers in the career area of her home. She informed me that a few days later an old acquaintance had called her out of the blue and offered her a fantastic new job.

Now, I'm not saying that this man met his wife solely because I feng shuied his house or that my client was offered a job purely because of the fresh flowers, but you would be surprised at how many times I hear similar stories from people whose places I have feng shuied.

This book is formatted systematically so that you can focus on one room at a time and it contains my fifty top tips for creating a happy home. The tips are a combination of the practical and easy-to-use Western style of feng shui and my own "Happy Home" additions, to help you have a healthy, harmonious and empowering environment, which will in turn act as a powerful support system for you as you go out into the world and do what you feel you are destined to do.

As you get started, you will be amazed how each tiny adjustment intuitively makes a lot of sense and has the capacity to make a really big difference in your life. One thing is for certain—whatever your personal circumstances are, you are really going to enjoy this process, because, above all, feng shui is really fun!

Love, Sophie

THE HISTORY AND DIFFERENT STYLES OF FENG SHUI

The art and science of feng shui has been practiced for thousands of years and over time it has evolved and changed forms. It originally began as a study practiced by priests and sages to discover the optimal place for a grave site. It was believed that if the ancestors were happy in their permanent resting places, it would help to ensure success for their family and country. This evolved into the study of the most auspicious placement of temples and palaces, and then feng shui came into use in houses belonging to the wealthy and eventually trickled down to the general public.

Many schools of feng shui exist, all of them with the same goal to improve your life by improving the energy of your environment. This book utilizes the simple and easy-to-use contemporary Western style of feng shui, called the Black Hat School, which uses the *ba gua* (you will learn more about this in tip #1). This particular style was originally brought to the United States by Grandmaster Professor Lin Yun, originates from the Black Sect of Tantric Buddhism and is an eclectic combination of Indian, Tibetan and Chinese teachings mixed with a Western approach to psychology, ecology and physiology.

The main idea behind this simple method is that it associates specific aspects of your life with specific areas in your home, using the front door as the point of orientation, known as the "mouth of chi" (the area where energy enters into the home). It is easy to use, very effective and does not require that you knock any walls down, spend large sums of money or sleep with your head in a compass direction that does not suit your space. Above all, it emphasizes the power of intention in creating the results that you want to see in your life.

Consider this: the closer a part of your environment is to you, the more impact it is going to have on you. With that in mind, read over the list of items below, which is arranged in order of closeness to you:

You

Your bed

Your bedroom

Your home

Your land

Your neighborhood

Your city

Your country

Your continent

Your world

Your universe

QUIZ: HOW HAPPY IS YOUR HOME?

Read each question and circle the answer that best applies to you and your home. If there are steps you can take to improve your home based on your answers, turn to the relevant tips in the book and start creating a happier home, one tip at a time!

Circle the answer that sounds the most accurate, then turn to page 118 for your results.

1. **How often do you clear out the clutter in your home?**

   A. I find it difficult to throw anything away and tend to be a bit of a hoarder.

   B. I clear out the clutter in my home once a year.

   C. I throw things out as I come across them and find they are no longer useful.

2. **If something is not working in your home (for instance, a bulb needs changing, a broken window or a door needs fixing), how long do you generally take to fix it?**

   A. I wait a number of months to a year and then get a few things done at once.

B. I leave it broken until I just can't take it anymore.

C. I fix it immediately.

3. **Which area do you feel you need to focus on most in your life right now?**

   A. Career and money.

   B. Relationships.

   C. Health.

4. **Have you had problems finding a partner while living in your home, or have you had problems in your current relationship since moving in?**

   A. Yes, I have found it difficult to date or communicate well with my current partner.

   B. I am not at a total loss, but the relationship area of my life could do with some improvement.

   C. No, I am very happy with the relationship part of my life and it is going very well.

5. **Do you have a bathroom located in any of these areas?**

   A. The back left-hand or right-hand corner of the house.

   B. The center of the house.

C. Opposite the front door, so you can see it immediately as you walk in.

6. **Since moving into your current home, have you found it easier to make money?**

    A. No, I have made less money.

    B. My money situation has remained the same.

    C. Yes, I have made more money since moving in.

7. **How would you describe your hallways?**

    A. Messy, dark and enclosed.

    B. Nice, but they could do with some work to improve the energy.

    C. Bright, warm and welcoming.

8. **Since moving into your home, how would you describe your social life?**

    A. I have become more withdrawn and have kept to myself.

    B. It is pretty much the same as it was before I moved into my present home.

    C. It has expanded and I have many more people in my life now.

9. **Where is your master bedroom located?**

   A. At the back of the house.

   B. At the front of the house.

   C. In the center of the house.

10. **If you work from home, how easy do you find it to concentrate?**

    A. I cannot seem to focus very well when I am sitting at my desk.

    B. Sometimes I find it easy and other times I struggle and find it much harder.

    C. I find it really easy to concentrate and usually get a lot done.

11. **What is the first room that you see when you enter your home?**

    A. The hallway.

    B. The kitchen, bathroom, dining room or a bedroom.

    C. The living room, office or den.

12. **Do you sleep well in your bed and bedroom?**

    A. No, I don't sleep that well.

B. My sleeping patterns are rather erratic. Sometimes I sleep well and sometimes I don't.

C. I get the perfect amount of sleep.

13. **When you stand outside your house or apartment and face your front door, which of the following emotions do you feel?**

A. Dreary or depressed.

B. Neutral.

C. Invited.

14. **If you were to draw a floor plan of your home, what would your floor plan look like?**

A. It would be rectangular or square in shape.

B. There are a few parts of the house missing that I would have to fill in on the floor plan to make it a square or rectangle.

C. It would be a rectangle with one or two extensions off the back or front of the house.

15. **When you walk in your front door, is the first thing that you see any of the following?**

   A. The back door or a huge glass window looking onto an area outside of the house.

   B. A wall or a cupboard.

   C. A staircase.

16. **How harmonious is the communication in your home?**

   A. There are a lot of unnecessary arguments.

   B. Sometimes we get along really well and other times there are clashes.

   C. It is a very harmonious household.

17. **How much have you grown and evolved as a person since you moved into the home that you are in?**

   A. I think I am the same as I always was.

   B. I have changed a bit. But I am not sure if it is for better or worse.

   C. I think that I have grown and evolved a lot as a person.

18. **How much has your career advanced since you moved in?**
   A. Not at all. I have lost my job or my way a bit and was better off before.
   B. My career has stayed the same.
   C. My career has really prospered since I moved in.

19. **How happy are you in your home and with your living situation?**
   A. I am desperate to move as quickly as possible and am working on it.
   B. It is fine for now but I know that I will soon want to move on.
   C. I am extremely happy where I live.

20. **Does your home have any of the following features?**
   A. Overhanging beams.
   B. Slanted ceilings.
   C. Ceiling fans or fireplaces.

1 How to Use and Place the *Ba Gua*

The school of feng shui explored in this book is based on the *ba gua*. The *ba gua* is a sacred map of the energetic world and it stems from the *I Ching,* which is an old method of reading energy used in many aspects of Chinese medicine and healing modalities.

The *ba gua* is usually presented as an octagon with eight sections, commonly know as *guas,* on the outside and an extra one in the middle, called the tai chi. The *ba gua* is a tool that will help you understand which parts of the environment within your home affect which areas of your life. Each part of the *ba gua* relates to a different life area. Each part (or *gua*) is full of meaning and one part of the octagon always affects another. You might want to focus on fixing your financial situation, for example, but all areas of your life will need to receive attention in order to achieve balance.

The *ba gua*

Health (Tai Chi)—*Physical Health.* Focus here if you want to increase your energy, your health and vitality. This area affects all others.

Wealth (Hsun)—*Abundance and Financial Status.* Focus here if you want to see an improvement in your financial situation and bring more money into your home.

Fame (Li)—*Fame and Reputation.* Focus here if you want to have a better reputation and be better known for what you do and who you are.

Relationships (Kun)—*Marriage and Partnership.* Focus here if you want to improve the relationship that you are in or if you want to find your life partner.

Children (Dui)—*Creativity and Children.* Focus here if you want to improve the health and well-being of your children and if you want to get pregnant.

Helpful People (Chien)—*Helpful People and Travel.* Focus here if you want to increase your circle of friends and your contacts in the business world.

Career (Kan)—*Life Path and Career.* Focus here if you want your career to improve, you want to get a promotion or find your life path.

Knowledge (Ken)—*Personal Growth, Knowledge and Spiritual Life.* Focus here if you want to become more self-aware and have more insight into others, as well as improve your knowledge in general.

Family (Jen). Focus here if you want to improve your relationships and the communication within your family.

Placing the *Ba Gua*

When you place the *ba gua* map (see the following illustrations), the bottom edge (the side that relates to knowledge, career and helpful people) should always be aligned with the entrance to one of the following three areas:

- **The Lot**—If you live in a house with a lot, place the *ba gua* on your plot of land with the bottom edge located where your driveway or gate crosses the street.

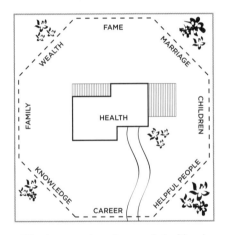

The *ba gua* placed on a plot of land

- **The House**—To get a general sense of the *ba gua* in your home, place the *ba gua* on your home floor plan with the front door to your home on the bottom edge. If you have more than one floor, consider the entrance to the landing on each level. If you encounter a wall, consider the entrance to be the point at which you see the whole room. If in doubt, apply the *ba gua* to each room individually.

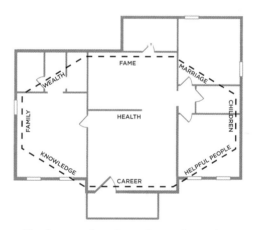

The *ba gua* placed on a house floor plan

- **A Particular Room**—To get a more specific picture, place the *ba gua* with the doorway to each room along the bottom edge of the *ba gua.*

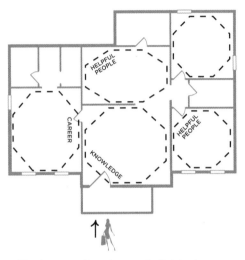

The *ba gua* placed on an individual room

If you have more than one floor to your house, align the *ba gua* with the top of the stairs when you go up and the bottom when you go down. If you encounter a wall when you enter the house or at the top of the stairs and have to turn right or left to walk into a space, then consider the entrance to be the point at which you see the whole room as you turn. On the ground floor you can use the main road as the entrance or the point where the whole room becomes visible as you turn. If you are in doubt, use both if you want, and always apply the *ba gua* to each room individually so that you cover all your bases.

2 Determine Your Feng Shui Goals and Intentions

A cure is any action you take in order to improve the feng shui in your home. The feng shui principles work best when you have a clear goal and intention. Make a list of the nine areas of the *ba gua* and write down how you want to improve each part of your life.

By discerning which areas of your life you need to work on, you can better focus your cures. If you want to be in a stable relationship, then you will focus your energy on the relationship areas of your home. If, on the other hand, you feel that you want a better job, then you will work on the career areas.

Remember that one area of your life always affects the others. For instance, if you are interested in relationships also focus on knowledge, as the more self understanding you have, the more likely you will be to get your needs met. If in doubt, focus on health. Being in the center of things, health reverberates out and affects everything surrounding it. When you physically place a cure, take a moment to see, hear and feel yourself achieving the goal that you have set for yourself in the life area that you are curing.

3 Cleanse Your Home with These 9 Simple Steps

Before you apply your feng shui cures, you need to clear out the clutter in your home. When you clean up your home, you rid it of stagnant and unhealthy energy. Most of us have too many things we don't actually need, and in getting rid of them, we create space for the cures to work.

1. If the idea of clearing out the clutter in your home seems overwhelming, then focus on one room at a time or one area in the room at a time, or even one drawer at a time, if necessary. As the famous saying goes, "Rome wasn't built in a day," so be kind to yourself, but do complete the task. The first step to shifting energy in your home and in your life is to make room for new and fresh energy to come in.

2. If you haven't used an item in the last six months, or a year at the most, then give it away to someone who might need it more than you. You will find enormous freedom in letting go of the objects and clothes that you really don't need anymore and you may even find the act of giving to those in need to be motivational.

3. Make sure you do not have an excessive amount of furniture, as too much bulk can stop the flow of chi around your home. There needs to be space for energy to flow and for you to move through your home with ease, without bumping into anything.

4. Do not just hide everything in a garage or an attic and pretend that you have gotten rid of it. The garage and attic are also considered parts of your home and you need to treat them as such.

5. Fix anything that is broken in your home. If you are having problems with the doors, windows, roof or any other part of the house structure, then fix it. You also want to make sure all the systems are in good working order and flowing well, which means the water, gas and electricity in your home.

6. If you think that your entire home or a particular room needs to be cleansed, you can wash the walls with water infused with nine drops of pure lavender or citrus essence in a bucket. This helps to cleanse the room of any old, stagnant energy.

7. Painting draws new energy into a home. If you have moved into a new home, then make sure that you paint the walls and deep clean the carpets to get rid of the energy of the previous occupants.

8. If you want to use color on one or all of your walls in different rooms, here are a few suggestions:

   Kitchen—White is a great color for cleanliness.

   Living Room or Family Room—Earth tones are very relaxing and grounding and have a capacity to draw people together. Blue or green also add life to these rooms.

   Bedroom—Peach, light blue and green are excellent choices.

   Children's Room—White, green or blue in your children's rooms will help them to flourish.

9. If you want to quickly remove the energy in your home after a few difficult weeks or months, then open all the windows and doors for a few hours and let the chi from outside flow through and clear your living space. You may also want to place a bouquet of fresh flowers in the middle of your home to enhance the cleansing process.

4 Prepare to Use the Feng Shui Cures

Feng shui cures are used to positively adjust the flow of chi throughout your home. When you transform the energy, you will experience a positive influence from your environment. By applying the cures from the feng shui toolbox, you can change whatever area of your life you desire.

If you want to improve an area of your life that is troubling you, or if you simply wish to turn an area of your life that is already good into something great, then you will use one or more of the cures in this book to achieve your goal. For example, you may use a mirror to draw energy into your relationship area in order to attract a new partner (see tip #6), or you may opt for a plant to grow your finances in the wealth area (see tip #8) or a crystal to help create clarity in your career (see tip #5).

Before you place the cures, make sure you take the following preliminary steps:

1. Stand in the doorway of each room and evaluate how the energy feels.

2. If there is any clutter, clear it out, whether you can see it in the room or it is hidden in the drawers or cupboards, because all objects take up energetic space. Fix anything that needs fixing in the room, clean where you need to clean and repaint if you need to.

3. Be very clear about what areas of your life you want to improve, and then place the *ba gua* map on each room.

4. Choose any cures that you want from your feng shui toolbox in order to:

   - Deactivate any negative influences that already exist. For example, you may want to soften a sharp corner, change the position of a bed to improve your sleep or turn your desk around so that you find it easier to work.

   - Enhance the energy around the room. For example, place a mirror to draw energy into a specific area or introduce a plant to bring in new life and growth. When you place the cure, clearly imagine that the improvement you seek in a particular area of your life has already happened.

5. Work on your own personal development and take practical steps forward to create the life that you want.

5 Use Toolbox Cure #1—Crystals

The biggest source of energy comes from the sun and its ability to create life. Crystals have an amazing power to activate the sun's energy; they bring in light from the sun and they can spotlight and bring a sense of expansion to any area that you place them in. The ones that I recommend you use are clear, faceted lead crystal spheres that are at least one-and-a-half or two inches in diameter. You can place them on a surface or hang them, depending on the location. If you hang them, follow the strict official feng shui way of displaying them, then hang them on a red string or ribbon cut into strips nine inches long or a multiple of nine. If you prefer to use clear wire rather than the traditional red ribbon because it is more aesthetically pleasing to you, then go for it. You can even put your own beads or stones on the wire if you want.

These faceted lead crystal spheres reflect natural sunlight and send out a colorful rainbow of light that can spread throughout a room. This light has the ability to:

• Shift stagnant energy.

- Energize a space and draw life into any nook or cranny that needs it.

- Interrupt energy if it is moving too fast.

- Balance out and disperse energy.

After you buy your crystal spheres, make sure that you rinse them clean under cold running water for a minute or two before you place them. When you place a crystal in a particular *gua* or area of your home, visualize what you want to happen in the corresponding part of your life. For example, if you put a crystal in the health area, imagine as you hang it or place it that it is drawing in more energy, vitality and health for you and your home. You might visualize your body healing, buying a smaller dress size or having more energy in general. You can always put a little mirror under a standing crystal so that it catches the sun and is activated, so you benefit from the beautiful rainbow colors across your room.

6 Use Toolbox Cure #2—Mirrors

Mirrors have an amazing capacity to:

- Draw new energy into a space and focus it in a particular area.
- Intensify what they reflect.
- Deflect energy.

When you buy a mirror, always have in mind that the bigger it is, the more powerful it will be. You do not want to use mirrors that are cracked or are tarnished in any way. Also avoid using mirror tiles, because when you look into them, your reflection will be broken into pieces.

Old mirrors are fine and can add character, but there should not be any scratches on the glass. You also do not want a mirror that is distorted in any way. For example, if a distorted mirror is placed in your wealth area, it can distort or tarnish your finances. If it's placed in a relationship area, it can do the same to your relationship. Also, be aware when you hang a mirror that it doubles the energy of whatever it reflects. If it reflects flowers, plants, a beautiful painting, a fish tank or a marvelous statue, then that is great. If it reflects the trash can or an electric pole outside, well, that's not so good.

When you hang a mirror, imagine it drawing energy into the areas of life you desire to expand. Make sure that it is hung so that you have a good bit of space above it and to the sides. If it cuts off your head when you look into it, it will affect your self-esteem, so make sure that the mirrors in the house are large enough to reflect the heads of the tallest and the shortest members of the household.

Mirrors really do create the illusion of space, and they are great in rooms that have a "missing piece," that is, that are not square or rectangular. If you have an L-shaped room, you can hang mirrors on the walls that "encroach" on the room to give the effect of pushing the walls back.

7 Use Toolbox Cure #3—Lights

Lights have an amazing way of:
- Lifting and activating chi.
- Filling in "missing areas" inside and outside the home.
- Spotlighting areas.

Lights do not have to be on all the time to have the effect that is needed in your home. However, light fixtures do need to be in working order all around the house. When you buy lights, consider ones that face up and lift up the chi in a room. If you have a slanted ceiling, an upward-facing light on the floor is appropriate, since it creates the effect of lifting up the slant (see tip #48). Do not use fluorescent lighting. Instead use full-spectrum lights where you can (see tip #32).

Lights are also indispensable if you want to spotlight an area or feature in your home, like your desk, which can help you focus more on work. When lit, candles and fireplaces also emanate great energy and have the ability to gather people together.

8 Use Toolbox Cure #4— Plants and Flowers

Plants are fantastic to have in your home as they:

- Symbolize new life.
- Symbolize growth.
- Emanate positive energy.
- Absorb pollution.

Place plants in the *guas* that you want to see grow. The best plants are those that grow upward, have round leaves and are not sharp like cactus. You want your plants to look healthy and full of life, so avoid any dried flowers and get rid of wilting flowers. Fresh-cut flowers send out very positive energy. Artificial plants do, too, so long as they look real. When you place the plant or flowers, imagine growth and new life in that particular *gua*.

Plants are also a great addition if you have carpeting in your home, as they help to absorb the toxicity in the carpet material.

9 Use Toolbox Cure #5— Water Features

Humans need water, and from the beginning of time we have constructed our homes near rivers, streams and oceans. Moving water inside and outside the home, when strategically placed, can:

- Draw prosperity into your home.

- Bring vitality into your home.

- Activate energy with its sound and motion.

- Help balance chi.

Water Fountains

A water fountain by the front entrance of your home is extremely beneficial (if you have the space for it). Make sure that the water is flowing toward your home rather than away from it, as you want the chi to flow inward. Get a fountain that suits the style and size of your home and the area in which you are placing it, and imagine increased prosperity and new opportunities entering into your home when you place it. The best fountains are ones where you can see the water flowing and the pool of water that it is flowing into. Flowing water inside or outside of your home in the career area can mean a flow in your work and finances.

Aquariums

Aquariums are great feng shui tools for lifting your mood. They bring vitality and energy to an area with their combination of fish, water and a bubbling pump. The fish circulate around the tank peacefully, which symbolizes an obstacle-free flow of life. Aquariums are known to generate new vitality, wealth and good fortune. That is why you see so many fish tanks in restaurants You need to keep the aquarium clean and the fish healthy and happy at all times. If any of the fish die, then replace them as soon as you can. Make sure you have a light in the tank and that the tank is big enough for all the fish to be happy as they grow. If they get too big for the tank, then let them loose in a small fishpond or take them back to the pet store. You do not want them to be stressed.

A fish tank in your career area is beneficial if you wish to bring in more money through your job or to set yourself up for a promotion. A fish tank in your wealth area is also great to bring in money.

Colorful fish are lovely and are a good option. If you want to use a very advanced feng shui technique, then have nine fish—eight goldfish and one black fish. If the black one dies, then it is said to eat up the negative chi that otherwise would have gone your way!

Swimming Pools, Lakes and Fishponds

Swimming pools, lakes and fishponds at the back of the house enhance the energy of the property and can increase the wealth of the occupants. However, there are a few principles that need to be observed when it comes to swimming pools. You want the pool to be in good proportion to the house. If it's too big, it can weaken the chi of the occupants and overwhelm the house.

The best shapes for swimming pools are round ones, such as ovals or kidneys. If the shape hugs the house, then the pool will have the effect of gathering and keeping wealth in the home. You don't want any sharp edges of the swimming pool pointing toward the house as this creates a poisoned-arrow effect and can stimulate accidents. To maintain the strongest balance, it is best when the pool is off to the side in back of the house rather than directly to the rear of it.

10 Use Toolbox Cure #6—Color

Color can improve the energy inside the home and change your mood.

Each color gives off a different energy and symbolizes different things. See page 34 for an illustration of the *ba gua* with corresponding colors and elements.

Black

Use black sparingly. It is a good color to use in your career, wealth and family areas to absorb energy.

Blue

Blue is the color of the intellect. It symbolizes spirituality and thoughtfulness. Represented by the water element, blue is good to use in the wealth, career and family areas.

Green

Green represents balance, new life, harmony and growth and it promotes healing. Use green in the wealth, family and fame areas.

Red

Red is the most positive color as it relates to joy, passion, power, protection and activity. Red is the fire element and is good to use in the relationship, knowledge and fame areas.

White

White is considered the color of purity, openness and innocence in the West. White is the metal element and is good to use in the children, helpful people and career areas.

Purple

Purple is the color of nobility and power. It is a very spiritual color. Purple belongs to the fire element and is good to use in your relationship, knowledge and fame areas.

Pink

Pink represents romance. It symbolizes love and the heart. Pink belongs to the fire and earth elements and is good to use in your relationship and knowledge areas.

Yellow

Yellow and the earth tones represent health and connection. Yellow is from the earth element and is good to use in the health, relationship, knowledge, helpful people and children areas.

Gray

Gray represents hidden things and can be used near the front door in your career, helpful people and children areas.

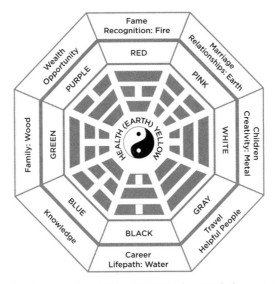

The *ba gua* with corresponding colors and elements.

11 Use Toolbox Cure #7—Mobiles

Mobiles rely on currents of air. They can:
• Move and stimulate energy.
• Clear stagnation in an extremely calm way.
• Balance and harmonize any chaotic energy.

Mobiles are great to use for softening any protruding corners or edges inside your home. They are also good for creating the illusion that a very high ceiling is not nearly so high.

If the mobiles are not in the path of natural air currents inside your home, you can tap them every once in a while to stimulate movement.

Placing flags and wind socks outside your home is also a great way to stir up energy. You can use them along the path to a front door that is located on the side of a house.

12 Use Toolbox Cure #8— Heavy Objects

Heavy objects can:

- Bring stability and calm to a space.
- Add weight and assist energy in moving downward.
- Have a grounding influence.

Since heavy objects help to ground a space, weighty statues are terrific in a garden. If your relationship is a bit rocky, then you can add a pair of stone statues to your relationship area inside your home. Also, a heavy statue can be added to fill in a missing area outside of your home (see tip #16).

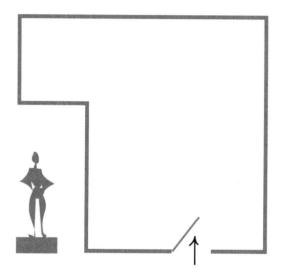

A statue fills in the missing area outside the home

13 Use Toolbox Cure #9—Sound

Sound can:

- Shift your mood.
- Lift your spirit.
- Help you relax.

If you want to relax your nervous system, then use harmonious and peaceful sounds. If you want to lift your energy, then use sounds or music with a strong beat.

Wind Chimes: Wind chimes create a harmonious sound and are used as a cure in feng shui. They can create new energy and stimulate new opportunities when hung inside or outside of your home.

Bells: Bells provide protection. For example, you can attach a bell to the door so that it rings whenever anyone enters.

Agitating Sounds: Unpleasant noises, such as lawn mowers and car alarms can agitate your nerves and make you feel tense. When possible, remove yourself from these sounds and maintain a balance by surrounding yourself with soothing, relaxing sounds.

14 Use Toolbox Cure #10— Bamboo Flutes

In China, bamboo is known to:
- Bring luck and support.
- Dissipate any negative energy.

Bamboo flutes are a very powerful cure used in feng shui. They represent strength, endurance and power.

If you are interested in using flutes, make sure that the ones you buy are actually made of bamboo and not cane. Bamboo is one of the strongest plants and its nodes and joints give the bamboo flute its own unique energy.

15 Find All the Missing Areas or Extensions in Your Home

In feng shui, homes and lots that are square or rectangular are best. Circles and octagons are good as well, but they tend to be quite rare. If your home is nearly a square or rectangle but not quite, then there is a way to discover if the irregularity in the shape is helping or hindering you.

In an irregularly shaped home, you will either have extensions or missing areas due to a lack of symmetry. Extensions are good, while missing areas are not. However, there are many easy ways to cure a missing area.

So how do you know if you have a missing area or an extension in your home or lot? If you already have a floor plan of your home drawn to scale, that's great. If you don't, then draw one yourself, doing your best to keep things to scale. You are searching for areas that look like they have had a bite taken out of them (missing areas) and areas where it appears that a "chunk" or a recessed space has been added on (extensions).

By definition a missing area is where *the gap* is less than half the width of the wall. It is an area of weakness and will need some curing.

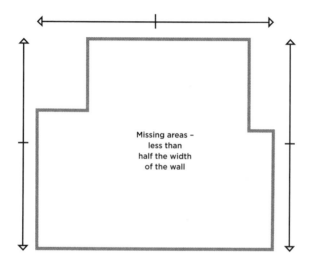

Missing areas –
less than
half the width
of the wall

Missing Areas: the home looks like it has bites taken out of it

By definition an extension is where the part of the home that *sticks out* is less than half the width of the wall. The energy in extensions is very powerful and extensions tend to bring more life opportunities into the areas in which they are situated.

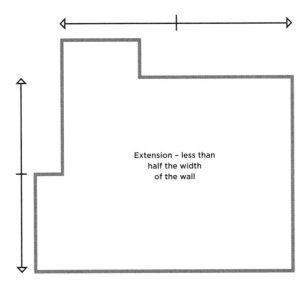

Extension – less than
half the width
of the wall

Extension: part of the home sticks out

16 Cure a Missing Area on the Outside of Your Home

To cure a missing area outside of your home, you will need to symbolically "complete" the shape of the house (see tips #12 and #15). By doing this, you will restore energy to the complete structure of your home. The best way to complete an area outside the house is to use one of these cures in the missing area to fill in the space.

1. Erect a large statue that is in good proportion to the house.

2. Plant a tree.

3. Plant a group of plants.

4. Install a light outside that will illuminate the top of the roof. (It doesn't have to always be on for it to work.)

5. Install a birdbath.

You can also mix and match these cures. The cure should be placed outside in a corner area that would symbolically complete the square or rectangular shape of your home.

17 Cure a Missing Area in Your Home

To cure a missing area on the inside of your home, you can:

1. Place a large mirror on both walls of the area that is missing. Make sure that they reflect something beautiful to enhance the cure (see tip #6).

2. Place a large faceted crystal in the interior corner, or a mobile, if you prefer (see tips #5 and #11).

3. Line the walls with healthy plants, as they will attract energy to the space and help make up for the missing area (see tip #8).

Even as you fix the missing area in one (or more) of the ways listed above, make sure that you strengthen the life area that it corresponds to in every other room of your home. For example, if the missing area you are fixing represents the relationship area in your living room, you will need to focus on strengthening the relationship areas in the other main rooms throughout your entire home (especially the master bedroom, the living room and the kitchen) to help make up for the missing area in that one room.

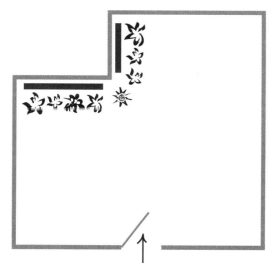

Plants, mirrors and a crystal fill in the
missing area inside the home

45

18 Cure a Missing Area on Your Lot

To cure a missing area on your lot, you can:

1. Erect a flagpole with a colorful flag at the corner of the missing part of the lot.

2. Mount a bright spotlight on a tall pole at the corner of the missing area.

3. Plant a hedge or a mixture of beautiful plants along the edge of the missing area.

4. Hang three flags or three spotlights, one at each of the three corners missing on your lot.

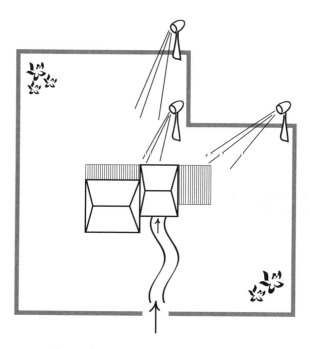

The missing area is cured with spotlights

19 Use the 5 Elements

The Chinese believe that everything in the environment is made of five elements, and that combining these elements in a variety of ways can help to create a balance in your environment. The elements are wood, fire, earth, metal and water and they are all used in feng shui to great effect. Each element has its own unique personality, energetic quality and color connected to it.

Wood (Family Area/Green)—Use the wood element when you want a new beginning or when you would like something in your life to grow and expand.

Fire (Fame Area/Red)—Use the fire element when you want more excitement and to experience a sense of expansion, an abundance of energy and recognition.

Earth (Health Area/Yellow)—Use the earth element to help stabilize, balance and ground an area in your life. It is especially beneficial in helping you become more centered.

Metal (Children Area/White)—Use the metal element when you want to improve your communication, stimulate projects and become more focused. It also has the effect of empowering your children.

Water (Career Area/Black)—Use the water element when you want more clarity in your life. It is effective in increasing the amount of people coming into your life and your cash flow. The water element also helps you to draw in peace of mind and a sense of stillness.

20 Combine the Elements to Make Your Cures Even More Powerful

The five elements play off of each other according to two different cycles, and when combined, their powers can become even greater. In the creative cycle, the elements feed each other so that each one enhances the next. In the destructive cycle, the elements consume each other.

The Creative Cycle
In the creative cycle, the elements interact as follows:

Water *feeds* Wood

Wood *fuels* Fire

Fire *creates* Earth

Earth *creates* Metal

Metal *creates* Water

How to Use the Creative Cycle

1. *Use the element itself:* You can put an element in its natural location. For example, if you want to increase your wealth you can put a plant (wood) in the wealth area or paint the

wall green or place a rectangular object in the space. In this way, you are using the object, the color or the shape that represents the element. Or you can use all three!

2. *Use the feeding element:* You can use the element that feeds the element in question—so you can put a water fountain in the wealth area, since water feeds wood.

3. *Use the element fed by:* You can use the element that is fed by the element in question—so you can put a red candle in the wealth area, since fire is fed by wood.

4. *Use all three:* You can also use all three of these options to set into motion a very strong cycle.

5. *Use all the elements:* You can always add all five elements to a space to create a sense of balance, wholeness and peace.

The Destructive Cycle

In the destructive cycle, the elements interact as follows:

Wood is *cut* by Metal

Metal is *burned* by Fire

Fire is *extinguished* by Water

Water is *absorbed* by Earth

Earth is *penetrated* by Wood

How to Use the Destructive Cycle

If any of the elements are situated in the natural location of a conflicting element, you might find that problems will arise. For instance, you don't want to put water fountains in the fame area (fire) of the house, because water destroys fire. There are several ways to fix conflicting elements:

1. Remove the element that is causing problems. For example, take the water fountain out of the fame area of your home.

2. Add more of the natural element to its natural home. In the fame area, for instance, you can bring in an object, color or shape that is a natural fit for fame.

3. You can counteract the offending element by adding a counter element to the area. For example, burn a candle in your fame area, as the fire will counteract the water element.

21 Bring More Opportunities through the Front Door

The front door is where energy and opportunities enter the home. It is often called "the mouth of chi," as the home takes in its nourishment through the front door much the same way we do through our mouths. And just as our health begins with what we eat, the health of our home begins with what passes through the front door and entryway. For this reason, your front door is one of the most important parts of your home, if not the most important part.

Ideally, you want your front door to be facing the street so that energy and opportunities can easily come off the road and to your door. However, if you don't have that luxury and your front door is hidden on the side of your home, then you can always put lights, plants, flags or even wind socks all the way from the street to the front door. Your goal is to direct the energy to your "hidden front door."

As you approach your front door, you should feel relaxed and happy. Your house number should be clearly visible from the street so it is easy to find you.

If you live in an apartment or condo, you may have to make your way through dark hallways in order to reach your front door. If this is the case, then make sure that between the entrance to the building and your front door there is a clear pathway. If you can, put a few plants along the corridor leading to your front door. If that is not possible, then perhaps you can put one or two outside your own front door, so that your energy is lifted when you see your home.

It is not necessary to change the color of your front door. Just make sure that it is in good condition. This means it shouldn't squeak, you don't have problems locking it, the handle isn't loose, the paint isn't peeling off, it doesn't have a broken bell and it doesn't scratch the floor as you open it. Doors that are not working properly or look worn-out can indicate that you are feeling worn down.

The only other kind of front door that you may want to fix is one that has a window in it, because the window can leave you feeling vulnerable and more easily broken into. If possible, replace the door with a solid wooden door or cover up the window so no one can see in.

22 Bring Extra Energy through Your Front Entrance with These 3 Tips

If you want to add extra energy to your front door and your space allows it, here are three ways that you can do it:

1. **Put a water feature at your front entrance**

   The front door and entranceway are both great areas for a dynamic water feature. The entranceway and career area are agreeably represented by the element water. The movement of water creates a relaxing sound, and the release of negative ions clears your head, brings in fresh energy and helps to bring about a balanced state of well-being. A fountain or waterfall helps to stimulate better health, more wealth and an increase in harmony for you and your family.

   The best fountains and waterfalls are those with a visible pool and freely flowing water. If the fountain is outside, make sure that its water falls toward your home.

2. **Put plants at your front entrance**

   Plants are excellent producers of healthy chi, so having two large potted plants on either side of your entranceway will help conduct healthy energy into your home. Plants with rounded leaves are generally better than those with pointed leaves. Try to avoid using cactus or dried plants.

3. **Put statues at your front entrance**

   If you are contemplating putting statues outside your front door, then consider foo dogs or lions as these powerful animals psychologically deter burglars. They are believed to have strong protective powers and have traditionally stood in front of Chinese imperial palaces, tombs and government offices to protect the people inside.

23 Disperse Energy from the Hallways throughout Your Home

If you imagine that the road outside your home is the ocean, then the path to your front door is a river that feeds from the ocean and the hallways are tributaries that branch off the river and flow into the rooms.

Thinking of it in these terms, you can understand that if there is a blockage at the front door or in the hallways (tributaries), then the energy and opportunities (water) entering into the rooms will dry up. So make sure that you keep your entranceway and hallways free of clutter.

You may love putting your coats, shoes, books, bikes and strollers by the door, and that is fine, so long as the space is tidy and nothing is blocking the door. You want the chi to have as much space as possible to flow freely through your home, and in turn to all the different areas of your life. The ideal entrance is uplifting and uncluttered, smells fresh, is pleasing to the eye and has a real sense of peace. Also it is well lit, open and spacious, with the capacity to draw you in and lead you to a comfortable place to sit, or it presents you with something beautiful to look at as you open the front door.

If you have the kind of hallways that are dark and cramped, they can take a toll on your general mood and health. Open up dark, narrow hallways by clearing out any clutter, bringing in some bright lights, using a crystal to disperse the energy and hanging mirrors. If there is a place for a plant or fresh flowers, then by all means use one or the other. However small your space naturally is, you can make the best of it.

24 Create Openness and Space at Your Entrance

If the first thing you see is a wall when you walk through your front door (as is common in many homes), you will always have a feeling of being blocked when you come home. To cure this, put up a large mirror so that it reflects whatever is outside of the door and creates a sense of space. You want to make sure that what is reflected is pleasing to the eye, because psychologically the mirror doubles the effect of whatever it reflects and you don't want that to be the trash cans!

If you are not greeted by a wall directly in front of you when you enter your home, but want to improve your entranceway, place an object that makes you the happiest to see when you first walk into your home. Is it a plant, an aquarium, a statue, a beautiful bright painting or a photo?

25 Understand the Influence of the First Room in Your Home

The first room that you see when you enter your house has a huge effect on your experience inside and outside of your home. Below is a description of some of the different rooms you may first enter and how they can influence you throughout the day.

Living Room or Den—If you walk directly into your living room or den, you may experience a sense of comfort and relaxation. Make sure you have a very comfortable place to sit down!

Study or Office—Walking directly into your office or study tends to make you more studious and ambitious in your career.

Kitchen and Dining Room—The kitchen is the room at the back of many homes. However, if the kitchen is the first room that you see or walk into, you may subconsciously want to eat the minute you arrive home, whether you are hungry or not! A dining room can have a similar effect. The best way to remedy this is to close off the entranceway so that you can't see the kitchen the minute you come in. You can also put a crystal over the position in which you cook at the stove to disperse the energy.

Bedroom—If your bedroom is right in front of you when you enter your house, then you may find that you are a bit lazy and want to lie down in bed the minute you get home. If this situation applies to you, then put a crystal halfway between the front door and the bed. Also make sure you keep your bedroom door closed.

Bathroom—If the first room that you see when you enter is a bathroom, then you definitely want to keep the bathroom door closed at all times. The view of a bathroom can have a draining affect on you and your finances, because the drains wash the chi away. If you wish to add an additional cure put a mirror on the front of the bathroom door, so that it reflects the energy away from the bathroom. (See tip #38 for more bathroom cures.)

What about Side Entrances?

If you park your car in a garage attached to your house and enter your home through the garage (or another side entrance), the above tips still apply. Make sure that the side entrance into the house is uncluttered and pleasing to the eye.

26 Cure a Staircase or a Back Door Opposite Your Front Door

Both a staircase and a back door opposite your front door affect the energy in your home but in different ways. Here's how and what you can do about it:

Staircase opposite the front door—If you have a staircase directly in front of the front door, your wealth and opportunities can suffer because as energy comes into your home, it travels up a few of the stairs and then back out again. If you find that this is the case, either put a plant at the bottom of the staircase or hang a faceted crystal between the front door and the bottom of the stairs, to slow the energy (chi) down. If you have a particularly large home and your budget allows, you can always hang a chandelier!

Back door opposite the front door—A back door directly facing the front door creates a wind tunnel effect with the flow of energy into and out of your home. The chi that comes in through the front door is forced to leave the space very quickly through the back door, without circulating throughout the house. The same is also true when there is a very large window opposite your front door. The location of the doors opposite one another *and* in the middle of the front of the house has the effect of splitting the house in two.

In both cases it is beneficial to hang a faceted crystal (or even a chandelier) in between the front door and the back door or window to slow the energy down and disperse it. You can also hang a sheer curtain up on the window opposite the front door to stop the energy from leaving the house as soon as it comes in, or use anything that you think will have the effect of preventing the chi from coming into your home and then going straight out.

27 Create the Ideal Floor Plan

If you are planning to buy a new home or are doing some remodeling, keep the following facts in mind:

The best rooms for the front of your home:

Office
An office at the front of your home keeps you connected to the outside world. From here you will find it easier to bring your business out into the world.

Guest Room
This room is suitable for the front of your home as this location prevents any of your guests from outstaying their welcome.

Children's Bedrooms
The front of your home is a good place for an older child's room as this location gives the child a feeling of independence.

The best rooms for the back of your home:

Master Bedroom

Without a doubt the master bedroom needs to be at the back of your home, if at all possible. This location is the most powerful, commanding one in your home. If your master bedroom is located at the front of your home, put a large mirror at the back of the house, directly in line with the master bed, so that you energetically draw the bed to the back of the house.

Kitchen

If your kitchen is at the front of your home, you will likely place a bigger focus on food and can gain weight more easily. You can cure this situation either by pulling the kitchen to the back of your home with the same mirror cure that was used for the master bedroom or by hanging a crystal or wind chime above where you would stand at the stove to balance the energy.

28 Cure the Center of Your Home

The front door may be the most important part of your home, but the center of the house plays a vital role. That is because the center of the house affects and is affected by the energy of all the other areas of the house and influences your physical, mental, emotional and spiritual health. Any cure that you do in the center vibrates out to all areas of the house, so it is really worth giving this area some extra attention.

Most rooms are just fine in the center of your home; however, there are a few that are going to need some help.

What to do if you have a bathroom in the center of your home

Usually there are three drains in the bathroom—one in the bathtub, one in the sink and one in the toilet, so the chi in the bathroom is naturally drawn down and this causes an energy drain. To fix this situation, keep your bathroom extremely clean and clutter free. Keep the toilet seat down and use plugs in the sink and bathtub when you are not using them. Make sure the air is fresh, and if you have any source of natural light, such as a skylight, then put a plant there. Also, hang a large crystal in the center of your bathroom and keep the door closed at all times. For a more comprehensive list of bathroom cures for this situation, see tip #38. A surefire feng shui cure is to mirror all four walls of the bathroom, which psychologically makes the bathroom disappear. However, that design feature may not be to your taste!

What to do if your master bedroom is in the center of your home

A bedroom in the center of your home can really be affected by the active swirling energy around it. If this is the case in your home, you may find that you have problems with sleeping and with your romantic relationships. If you find that this is happening, put a large mirror on the back wall of your home, directly in line with your bed, so that you psychologically draw the bed into a safe position at the back of the house. Also, you can hang a faceted crystal in the middle of the ceiling above your bed to stabilize the energy of the room.

What to do if you have a spiral staircase in the center of your home

A spiral staircase creates a flow of energy that bores down into the earth, which can result in a loss of money or health. The best cure for this is to lift the chi back up by hanging a large faceted crystal from the ceiling above the staircase.

What to do if you have a cupboard in the center of your home

If there is a cupboard in the center of your home, you need to make sure that it is clean and tidy. Put a crystal in the middle of the cupboard to emanate positive energy all around.

What to do if you have a fireplace in the center of your home

If you have a fireplace in the center of your home, make sure you put a mirror above it so that your health doesn't go up in smoke. The mirror has the effect of balancing out the fire element. You can also put a plant or a few plants by it to bring life and balance to the area. Do your best not to use the fireplace too much.

29 Improve Your Living Room with These 9 Simple Steps

The living room is well situated in any area of the house. It is a room that we like to relax in and hang out with friends in, and for many of us it acts as a television room or den. In order to improve it…

1. **Remove unneeded objects and furniture**—Stand in the doorway of your living room and get a sense of how the energy feels in the room. Does it feel old or new? Are there too many books? Is there an excess of furniture? You want to make sure that your living room isn't cluttered with too many objects. All objects have a vibration and you need to have space to relax and think. (See tip #3 for more on cleansing your home.)

2. **Color the walls for relaxation**—Make sure that the room is warm, comfortable and welcoming. If it needs a new coat of paint or if the walls need to be washed, do not hesitate to do so. White, earth tones or gentle pastel colors work well on living room walls. When you decorate, think about what makes you want to relax.

3. **Place chairs in the power position**—Place your seating in the power position. This entails arranging the sofa so that it affords a good view of the entrance to the room and doing your best not to place any piece of furniture with its back to the entrance, as this can create a feeling of vulnerability. If you have no choice but to arrange the sofa with its back to the entrance, due to the layout of your living room or the size of it, then you can always put a table behind the sofa to protect it from the chi coming in through the door and some plants on the table to dispel any negative energy. You can also put a mirror on the wall in front of the sofa so that it reflects the entrance and you can see who is coming in behind you when you are on the sofa.

4. **Place your coffee table by the couch**—I always recommend putting a coffee table in front of your couch, as you are much more likely to sit there than any other place in the living room. The coffee table has the effect of grounding the space and centering a conversation.

5. **Minimize walkways**—If you have walkways in between your furniture, it is going to be much more difficult to relax when people walk in front of you and past you. If your living room layout demands this type of setup, it is much better for you to place the furniture in small groups on either side of a

single walkway so that you are not constantly disturbed by passersby!

6. **Don't give the television center stage**—If you have a television in your living room, don't make it the center of attention. The living room is for entertaining, good conversation and the exchange of ideas. You may want to put the television in a TV armoire with doors so that you can keep it out of sight when you aren't using it.

7. **Use lots of plants and flowers**—A fresh plant is great to have in a living room. It freshens the air and clears away some of the electromagnetic fields that are generated by the television screen and other electronics. Also, fresh flowers represent new life and they look fabulous on a coffee table or sideboard.

8. **Pick your wall decor carefully**—Make sure that the paintings or photos that you have up in your living room are warm and inviting to look at. The best subjects for paintings are nature and people.

9. **Use low shelves**—Make sure that your shelving units are low in the living room, especially if you have a small space. You don't want to feel overwhelmed by shelving or have it take up a huge amount of space and make the room feel smaller.

30 Use the *Ba Gua* in Your Living Room

The living room is a perfect room in which to employ the *ba gua*. Here's how:

1. **Healing Your Life Areas**—Mentally place the *ba gua* map over your living room. You need to pay special attention to the facets of your life that you are working on and the areas in your living room that correspond to those facets. If it's your relationship, then look to see if the back right area of your living room is cluttered, dusty and needs some life. If it's your family dynamic you want to improve, notice what the left middle part of the room looks like. Does it need a plant, a crystal or something else to balance out the energy?

2. **Bring Chi into the Corners**—You want to draw chi into every corner of your living room, so make sure that they are all bright and uncluttered. You can enhance the vibration of those areas with a plant, a mirror, a bright painting, a light, a crystal or anything else in your feng shui toolbox that you think will help illuminate what you want to draw attention to in your life.

3. **The Power of a Mirror**—A mirror is always good for chi when it is strategically placed in a living room. Place one above an existing fireplace, for instance, or in an area to which you want to draw attention. Also, remember that if your living room is an odd shape, you can add mirrors to open up the missing area (see tip #17).

31 Cure Electromagnetic Fields

A major cause of negative energy inside of the home is all the electrical and electronic devices that we use. These include radios, computers, electric stoves, hair dryers, lights, televisions, microwave ovens, smoke detectors, lighting, cell phones and more. The amount of electrical and electronic equipment that affects our natural state is endless.

There has been a great deal of research into how increased exposure to electromagnetic fields (EMFs) can weaken the immune system, damage the body and create sleep disorders, as well as increase the possibility of developing ADD and nervous disorders. At any opportunity move electrical and electronic items as far away from your body as possible and do some research to find some effective EMF protection devices, especially for your computer and television.

Here are some other actions to take in your home:

1. Use a landline at home rather than a cell phone. This will reduce your exposure to electromagnetic radiation (EMR).

2. I know it sounds contradictory, but do not rest your laptop computer on any part of your body, especially your lap, for long periods of time. Instead place the laptop on a lap table or, better yet, an ordinary table!

3. Keep your alarm clock about thirty inches away from you when you sleep. A battery-operated one is better for you than one that plugs in.

4. Do not use your microwave oven much, or better yet, get rid of it completely. Stop radiating your food, as microwaves destroy many nutrients.

5. Do not use an electric blanket; use a hot water bottle instead.

6. Be aware of what is behind the wall where you sleep. If it is an electrical appliance, move it if you can.

7. Do your best to limit the use of your hair dryer. If you have to use it every day, then do it quick!

8. If you have to sit for long periods of time in front of your computer without taking breaks, then get a radiation shield for your monitor.

9. Do not store your cell phone in any of your clothes pockets. This will help to reduce your body's exposure to EMR.

32 Use Full-Spectrum Lighting

Use energy-saving lightbulbs and restrict your use of fluorescent lights, which emit a large amount of electromagnetic pollution. Fluorescence gives off mainly a yellow color, rather than the recommended full spectrum of the rainbow (which is what full-spectrum bulbs produce, simulating sunlight).

Researchers have proven that fluorescent lights cause headaches, eye strain, sleep disorders, depression, learning disorders, skin cancer, dermatitis and many more illnesses. Fluorescent light also affects hormone levels and stress levels and has the capacity to make you tired and angry. A study conducted in the 1960s showed how mice lived for eight months under fluorescent lighting and twice as long when exposed to natural daylight. So help to protect your health in your home and use full-spectrum lightbulbs.

33 Use These Simple Ideas to Improve Smaller Spaces

When you live in a smaller space, you want to ensure that it feels as open as possible. Here's how:

Avoid Clutter: Throw out the stuff that you don't need, and put anything that won't fit in a small space into storage.

Use Mirrors and Crystals: Use large mirrors to open up the space and strategically hang a few crystals to create a feeling of expansion.

Use Plants and Nature: Make sure that you have some plants in your home to keep the air clear and open the windows whenever you can. Photos of nature bring in outside energy.

Define the Space in Your Studio: If you are in a studio, keep the space divided up to simulate separate rooms. Have fun designing the space and separating areas with screens, tall plants, bookshelves and curtains so that the space is sensibly divided. Keep in mind that ideally you do not want to look at your refrigerator while you sleep or have your bookshelf and electronics too close to your bed.

34 Bring New Life into Your Dining Room with These 9 Essential Steps

In a large home, the dining room is often the most unused room, and yet in many ways it can be one of the most important. Traditionally, dining rooms are a place to connect with your family and friends. The dining room is one of the rooms in your home that really needs to be made warm, calm and inviting. If you don't have a formal dining room, then do your best to make whatever area you choose to dine in separate and inviting.

1. **Use a dimmer switch:** Make sure that the space is bright and that soft colors, like beige and yellow, predominate. Put a dimmer switch on your light so you can change the mood to help you relax after a long day or when you have friends over.

2. **Create space for guests:** Make sure that there is enough space for each person to comfortably pull out a chair and sit around the table. Limit the amount of decorations that you have, as you don't want the dining room to be cluttered or cramped in any way.

3. **Use crystals:** Keep the flow of energy through the dining room slow but consistent. A crystal chandelier over the table will

help that happen and at the same time it will help to balance the energy of the room. Or you can use a large faceted crystal, which will also help to spread chi throughout the room. This is particularly useful if the dining room features two doors opposite each other, where energy is running in and out rather quickly.

4. **Hang a mirror:** A mirror in the dining room is always a great addition. In feng shui, a mirror overlooking the table is beneficial for wealth creation, as it doubles the food laid out, symbolically doubling your money. The mirror also helps to expand the space and keep the chi moving.

5. **Allow everyone to be seen:** If you have candlesticks, a vase or other tall decorative elements on the dining room table that limit your view of those seated, then put them off to the side when using the table so that everyone can easily see one another, otherwise they will stop the conversation from flowing. The same can be said for bottles of wine or water. Put them at one end of the table so that they do not block anyone's view, or even better, put them on a sideboard or side table.

6. **Arrange guests for a balanced ambiance:** When you have a dinner party, guest placement can be quite important. If one of your guests is usually not that chatty, put him in a power position by seating him in the chair farthest from the door,

as this will encourage him to talk more. In the same way, if a guest tends to talk too much, put her closest to the door, with her back to it. This should help to quiet her down. Such seating arrangements will help you to create a balanced dinner party ambiance, and a fun and relaxing party.

7. **Cure a beam over the table:** A beam over the dining room table isn't particularly good feng shui and it can affect your career and money areas. If this is the case in your home, you have a few options. You can either move the table, paint the beam to match the ceiling or put bamboo flutes at each end of the beam.

8. **Use your favorite place settings:** Make sure you use your favorite place settings for yourself. Don't just reserve them for guests. Maybe use them when you have a romantic dinner with your partner or on the odd occasion when the whole family gathers for a meal.

9. **Make sure you have a centerpiece:** Keep a bowl of fruit or flowers in the middle of the dining room table when it is not being used. Both help to ground the table and draw health into the room.

35 Place Large Furniture Pieces in the Commanding Position

The commanding position principle is age-old. In primitive times humans used to set up homes where they would be protected by hills or mountains. This same concept can be applied today both inside and outside of the home.

When it comes to the placement in your home of major pieces of furniture, like a bed, desk or sofa, keep in mind that the best place for them is in the all-important commanding position, which means that when seated or lying…

1. You have the widest possible view of the room, so that you have a sense of overlooking the space.

2. You can see the entrance clearly.

3. You have a solid wall behind you for support.

4. You are as far from the door as possible.

5. You are not in the direct line of the door. (You do not want to be hit by fast-moving chi as it enters the room.)

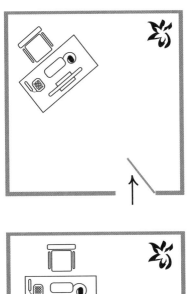

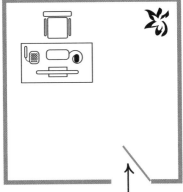

Desks in the commanding position

These five aspects will help you to be in command of your life. However, you don't want to be too rigid when it comes to placing furniture in the commanding position. For example, a bed or a desk with a huge window behind it is not such a good idea even if it affords a wide view of the room. Sitting or lying under a slanted ceiling or a beam is not a good idea even if you have a solid wall behind you. There are always ways to rectify the situation if furniture cannot be comfortably placed in the commanding position. For example, you can hang a mirror so that you can easily see the door when you are sitting at your desk, sitting on your sofa or lying in bed.

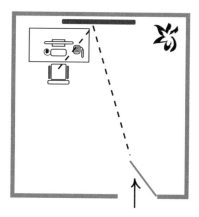

A mirror allows you to easily see the door from the desk

36 Improve the Energy in Your Child's Bedroom

Here are some simple ways to improve the energy in your child's bedroom:

1. **Where to position the bed:** Make sure that your child's bed has a headboard and is in the commanding position in the room (see tip #35). Make sure you don't put the headboard under a window, as your child will have problems sleeping.

2. **All legs aboard:** Make sure that your child's bed fits him. His legs must not hang off the bottom of the bed! You don't want to stunt your child's emotional, mental and physical growth.

3. **The problem with bunk beds:** Bunk beds limit the space in which the chi can circulate above your children's heads while they sleep. The child on the top bunk will not feel grounded and the child who is sleeping underneath will likely begin to feel cramped and stifled. If you already have bunk beds or have just bought them, try to vary who sleeps on the top and bottom bunk and if you can afford to, restrict their use to a short period of time.

4. **What colors to paint your child's room:** The best color for a child's bedroom is white. Light pastel colors are also good as these colors promote growth and a sense of calm. Bold colors can promote hyperactivity.

5. **Pay particular attention to artwork:** Make sure that the images and artwork in your child's bedroom are all positive, happy and friendly.

6. **Where to place mobiles:** Do not place mobiles over the area where your child rests her head when she sleeps. It is better to hang it above the foot of the bed, or use it to soften a corner that is sticking out.

7. **Avoid beds that have storage underneath:** If you already have one, then use the space for neatly storing extra bedding or seasonal clothes. Avoid storing toys or books there as your child will either have problems getting to sleep, have restless nights or always be tired.

8. **Keep the room tidy:** Too much clutter in a child's room can prevent them from thinking clearly, so clear out any unused toys, books and clothes.

9. **When to use a plant:** Keep a large plant in the room to keep it fresh. Plants also absorb the formaldehyde in the carpet.

10. **No TV or computer in the bedroom:** If your child needs a computer for studying and it sits on his desk, then divide the work and sleep areas of the room with a screen or curtain so that he doesn't have trouble getting to sleep.

11. **Where to use crystals:** A crystal in your child's window can help her become more creative. When the sun hits the crystal, the rainbow colors create a wondrous effect as they bounce off different parts of the room. You can also use a crystal to soften a corner that is sticking out, or hang one in the middle of the room to help balance out the energy in the whole space.

37 Make Your Home Office More Effective

A home office needs to be a place of productivity. Here are six simple ways to make yours as productive a place as possible:

1. **Select the Best Room for Your Office**
   The best place for a home office is at the front of your house so that you can feel part of the outside world. The only exception to this is if you are a writer or an artist that needs peace and quiet—in that case the back of your house is also a good choice. You certainly do not want the home office to be in the center of your house, as it has the potential to dominate and make your work life seem more important than your home life.

2. **Decorate for Productivity and Inspiration**
   You need a tidy office with very little clutter so that you have the space in which to think freely, generate new ideas and make room for new business to come in. Make sure that you can move freely around the room, and that any paintings or photos on your walls inspire you to work hard.

3. Position Your Desk in the Best Place

Your desk is like your bed in your bedroom—you need to place it in the commanding position (see tip #35). You'll find that you work much better in this position and it will help you be in control of your work and new developments. If you can't face the door, put a mirror up on the wall opposite the door so that you can see the door reflected in it from your desk. If one side of your desk is up against a wall, pull it away so that you can easily get behind your desk from either side.

4. Pay Attention to the Quality of Your Desk and Chair

It is always ideal to buy a new desk so that it doesn't have anyone else's energy on it. If you do buy a used desk, make sure to give it a really good cleaning with a bucket of water to which nine drops of lavender or citrus oil have been added.

When you buy a new desk, take note that the best desks have a full front panel, one that extends all the way to the floor. These provide complete protection and enhance your status.

As for your chair, the ideal thing is to get a new one or to inherit one from someone who had success in it. If you decide to buy a new chair, go for one that extends up your back at least to your shoulders, as this gives you a feeling of strength and security.

5. **Be Smart about Lighting and Electrical Equipment**

The typical office contains a great deal of electrical equipment and EMFs. One way to absorb some of the electromagnetic waves is to have a large plant in the room to soak up any toxicity in construction materials and the formaldehyde in carpets.

Make sure that you have a bright light with a full-spectrum energy-saving lightbulb on your desk.

6. **Use the *Ba Gua* in Your Home Office**

You can place the *ba gua* on your desk, with the entrance corresponding to where your stomach meets the desk. Put your phone in the wealth area, so that when it rings, it brings in more business, and put your light in any area that you want to brighten or activate.

The home office is a great place to focus on the wealth, helpful people, relationship and career *guas* to help promote a busy and profitable work life.

38 Fix Your Bathroom for Better Health and Wealth

Bathrooms are known to affect your health and wealth and they tend to get a bad rap because, due to the drains in the sink, toilet, bathtub and shower, there is a downward flow of chi, which forces the energy to drop rather than rise. This draining effect tends to weaken whatever part of your home the bathroom is located in. However, there are a number of cures that you can perform to lessen the impact of the bathroom on your home.

1. Keep the bathroom door closed at all times! If you have problems with other people in the house complying with this rule, then you can always put a spring on the door so that it automatically shuts.

2. Hide bathroom drains when not in use so that energy does not drop down. This means that you want to keep the toilet seat down and use stoppers in the sink, shower and bathtub.

3. Hang a full-length mirror on the outside of the bathroom door so that it reflects out and has the effect of making the bathroom vanish (since the mirror reflects whatever is outside

of the bathroom). The mirror will deflect the chi away from the bathroom. This works only if you keep the bathroom door shut.

4. If your bathroom has natural light, then place a plant in it. This is going to help balance out the excess of water energy with some wood energy. At the same time the plant will keep the atmosphere fresh and clean. You want to use plants that lift chi by growing upward, like bamboo. If you don't have a window in your bathroom, then you can always use an artificial plant, so long as it looks real. I always recommend placing a plant on the back of the toilet if possible. If there is no space there, select another part of the bathroom, since a plant will have a beneficial effect no matter where it is placed.

5. A very powerful cure is to install a small (preferably at least three inches in diameter) round mirror on the ceiling directly above your drains, which has the effect of drawing up the chi that would otherwise drop down.

6. It's very important to put a lot of effort into decorating your bathroom with photos, plants, art, candles—whatever makes you happy. Remember that your goal is to lift up the chi and make your bathroom as inviting as possible.

7. The best location for a toilet is behind the door or a low wall, so that it is not the first thing that you see when you open the

door. If you can see the toilet when you stand in the doorway, hang a faceted crystal halfway between the toilet and the door to balance the energy.

8. The ideal position for the bathtub is with the taps closest to the door so that you can see who enters. If you do not have this luxury, then put a small mirror up so that when you are bathing, you can easily see if someone enters the bathroom.

9. The most ideal flooring to have in a bathroom is wooden floorboards, ceramic tiles or linoleum.

39 Cure the Location of the Bathrooms in Your Home

The ideal place for a bathroom is away from all the other activity in your home and in an area to which you feel you can retreat. Some locations are less favorable than others; however, unless you are building your own home, you generally do not get to choose where your bathrooms are located. The family, children and helpful people areas are ideal locations for a bathroom, and hopefully these areas will have plenty of natural light.

The Center of the House: This is the least favorable area for a bathroom to be located, since the center of your home is in direct relation to all the other parts of it. If your bathroom is located in the center of your home, the most advanced cure is to mirror the four interior walls of the bathroom. If mirrors are not possible or do not quite work with your decorating style, then use some of the cures in tip #38 to really make the bathroom look beautiful and feel welcoming.

The First Room Seen: A bathroom in this location can really draw the incoming chi and opportunities through the front door and then straight down the bathroom drains! The most powerful cure in this particular situation is to keep the bathroom door closed and to hang a full-length mirror on the outside of the door. Combine that with keeping the toilet seat down and the bathtub, sink and shower drains closed when not in use.

The Relationship Area: If you have a bathroom in your relationship area, you may notice that you are having communication issues in an existing relationship, that you have short-lived relationships or that you never seem to meet anyone. If this is the case, then apply some of the cures in tip #38. In addition, you may want to add two identical stone statues to your bathroom.

The Wealth Area: If you have a bathroom in the wealth area, you might find that you are having problems making money or that money comes in easily but quickly goes straight out. Apply some of the cures in tip #38 if this is your situation.

40 Fire Up Your Stove to Improve Your Health and Wealth

The ideal location for the kitchen is at the back of your home, as the back of your home is much calmer and more secure than the front. This location also protects the sensitivity of the stove, which is one of the most important and powerful parts of the home. In feng shui the stove represents your health, your wealth, your relationships and your entire well-being.

1. **The Position of the Stove:** Ideally, you want the stove to be in the commanding position, so that you have the widest possible view of the room and can easily see the doorway from the stove. However, not many kitchens have this type of layout. Ordinarily, the stove is pushed up against a wall, so that when you are cooking, your back is to the room. The best way to counteract this, is to put a large mirror that is the width of the stove behind the stove so that when you are cooking, you can see if anyone is behind you. Shiny stainless steel will also do the trick. Reflecting your burners is also said to double your wealth!

If there is no space for a mirror at the back of your stove, then the best thing to do is to put a standing mirror on the counter or even hang a mirror on the wall next to the stove so you can glance over to see who is behind you.

2. **The Condition of the Stove:** Your stove needs to be in tip-top condition, which means the light, clock, fan, knobs and, most important, all the burners on your stove work at all times. Don't use just the front burners, but rotate, using them all. Burners represent the wealth-generating potential of your home.

3. **The Cleanliness of the Stove:** Make sure that the stove is clean at all times and that the surfaces are free of old food, which has stale energy attached to it. A dirty stove can indicate that you are tired and depressed.

41 Improve the Health of Your Kitchen

Here are nine easy solutions for a healthier kitchen:

1. **Clutter Free:** Keep the kitchen clutter free and make sure that you actually use everything that is stowed away in your cupboards. The kitchen is a hub of activity, a place to enjoy food and conversation. The atmosphere should be fresh, warm and bright.

2. **The Stove Beside the Fridge:** If your stove and refrigerator are next to each other, then you want to create a symbolic distance between them. A great deal of conflict is generated when mixing the energy of the hot fire element, represented by the stove, and the cold water element, represented by the refrigerator. To fix this you can either put a mirror on the refrigerator facing out toward the stove, which symbolically pushes the refrigerator away and expands the stove area, or you can place a faceted crystal between the two to create a balance. Also, if you have the space, you can put some plants between the fridge and stove to create an energetic barrier.

3. **The Sink:** Keep the sink clean and unblocked, with a stopper in it when you are not using it. Make sure that the garbage disposal unit is working well if you have one.

4. **Knives:** Keep your knives safely away in a drawer or in a knife block.

5. **The View:** Hang a crystal in the kitchen window as it attracts energy from outside and serves to deflect any negativity if you have an unsightly view out of your window.

6. **Microwave Ovens:** Restrict the use of microwave ovens as they distort the molecular structure of your food and destroy many of its nutrients.

7. **Under the Sink:** Be aware of what poisons are located underneath your sink. If you were to take all the cleaning products that you have under your sink and pour them all into a bucket, you would likely find a huge amount of poisonous chemicals. Many of these products are extremely toxic. They are dangerous to inhale or may cause an adverse reaction if they get on your skin, aside from the fact that they are extremely poisonous if swallowed. There are so many ecologically friendly products on the market now that it makes much more sense to replace the toxic products you currently own with ones that are much safer to have in your home. They might vary in price slightly, but it is definitely worth limiting the amount of poison that you keep under your sink, and if

you want to keep it cheap, you can always use products like baking soda, borax, white vinegar and cornstarch.

8. **Inside Your Refrigerator:** If you tend to buy food in packets or jars, then get into a habit of reading what is on the label. The more real ingredients in a product, the better it is for you. Conversely, the more a product label reads like a chemistry experiment, the worse the product is for you. If you don't know what a word on the label means, then look it up. If there are additives in something, be aware that they won't provide your body with the nutrients it needs for health or energy. As a rule of thumb, you will tend to find more additives in foods that have low nutritional value. If you find you really can't do without your favorite food, then try to find a more natural alternative.

9. **Your Water:** If you drink your tap water without filtering it, then it would certainly be wise to find out exactly what is in it. If there is any chlorine in it (and any other hidden unwanted substances), which there very likely is, then filter it. You need to drink a large amount of water each day to replenish your cells, and it is important to make sure that you are feeding your organs pure water, not a continuous dose of chlorine. You can install a water filter on the kitchen faucet or under your sink, or simply use a water filter pitcher that you keep on your sideboard or in the refrigerator.

42 Find Your Ideal Home

Just as feng shui can be applied to your current home, you can also use it when looking for a new home. Finding your ideal home will take time and commitment. Here are a few ways in which you can become clear on what you want and speed up the process of getting it.

1. **Act As If:** Clear the clutter out of your home as if you are moving. It doesn't matter if you have found a place to move into or not; just imagine that you have and you have to do the first part of the moving process. Organize yourself and get rid of everything you are not planning to take with you. Use this time to give away or throw out anything that you haven't used in the last year. In doing this, you are essentially letting the universe know that you are serious about moving, which in turn may help you find a new home. Also, by doing all this earlier on, you are going to find the moving process so much easier when it's actually time to move.

2. **Determine Your Priorities:** List the five things that are most important to you in a new home. If you are married or have

a partner, then you both need to write down your top five so that you are clear about what you are looking for. Ask yourself questions like, do I want to be able to walk to shops? Does it have to be quiet? Do I need a garden? Do I want high ceilings? Does the house need to be light and bright? Write everything down, and then, if you are moving by yourself, look at the top three things you cannot in any way do without. These are your essential needs. If you live with a partner, decide which are the top three things you both cannot do without. It is unrealistic to think that you will get everything you want in a new home, but if you can get your most important needs met, that is a great start.

3. **Project Forward:** Visualize what you want and where you see yourself living. Imagine yourself there. How do you want to feel when you live there? What do you want to be able to say to your family and friends about your new place? Visualize what you might see on the inside. The more you are clear in your mind's eye about what you are looking for, the more likely you are to find it. And again, if you are moving with a partner, then sit down and visualize your home together.

4. **Trust Your Gut:** Carefully note your feelings when you first walk into a place. Did you have problems finding it? If you did, then other people will. Do you feel that you can breathe easily

when you walk into the space? Can you see that you will be productive there? Can you imagine how you would decorate it? When you go to look at any potential new homes, trust your gut reaction. If it feels right when you enter, it probably is. If it doesn't, then don't try to make it fit, and keep looking until you do find what you want. Be patient.

5. **Ask the Right Questions:** Each home that you live in has its own energy, so find out why the people who lived there previously are moving. This will give you a clue as to how well they fared in the house before deciding to move. If you ask these sorts of questions, you will get a good idea of the energy of the home, which is important, as that same energy will affect you as well, until you consciously change it.

43 Make the Master Bedroom a Place of Calm

The master bedroom is perhaps the most important room in your home. It is where you withdraw to rejuvenate in order to come out into the world refreshed. As it is the place where you spend the most amount of time, if you can really replenish your energy in your bedroom properly, you will emerge into the world in a more balanced and peaceful way. If your bedroom is wired with electronics or your bed is placed in a weak position, you will likely feel unbalanced and drained. If you have children and your bed and bedroom nourish your energy, then as the caretaker, you can much more easily nourish your children's energy.

Follow the suggestions below to make sure that you are getting the most out of your bedroom:

1. **The Commanding Position:** The best place for a master bedroom is at the back of your home, in the commanding position, where it is quieter, more peaceful and protected. If you imagine drawing a line horizontally through the middle of the house, behind that line is the most ideal place for a master bedroom.

2. **Electronics:** The master bedroom is not a place for you to be "wired," so take all the electronics out, including your computer and television, and put them in another room. If this isn't an option, then at least make sure to keep your computer turned off and your television covered when not in use.

3. **Books:** Make sure you have only a few books in your bedroom so that you are not overstimulated while you are trying to rest. If you have a few books by your bed that you are reading, that is fine. Just make sure to keep the home library outside of the bedroom.

4. **Clutter Free:** Keep your bedroom simple, balanced and calm with no unnecessary furniture cluttering up your space. Go through your closets annually and give away any clothes that you have not used in the last year. Do not store anything under your bed!

5. **Plants:** To help keep the environment calm and the atmosphere fresh, keep a large plant in your bedroom. A good place for it is in the relationship area. Also, you may want to use freshly cut flowers to brighten up the room and bring fresh energy into your relationship.

6. **Pictures and Photos:** Remove any photos of family members from your bedroom, apart from any that you have of you with your partner. It is not ideal to have photos of family members

staring at you when you are attempting to have a romantic moment. You also do not want any photos of you by yourself in the bedroom. If you do have pictures in your bedroom, make sure that they are relaxing. Images of nature are preferable. The images in your bedroom should add to the sense of calm that you are creating throughout the room.

44 Fix the Position of Your Bed

Part of the reason why the bedroom is so important is that it houses your bed, which is where you spend a good deal of your time. The bed assists your ability to rejuvenate throughout the night and therefore affects your health as well as your love life.

1. Just as you want your bedroom in the commanding position, so, too, do you want your bed in a place in the room where you feel completely safe and in control. This means that it needs to be as far from the bedroom door as possible. Ideally, it should be placed where you have the widest possible view of the whole room and where you can easily see the bedroom door. If you cannot easily see the door from your bed due to the room layout, then make sure to put a mirror up on the wall opposite the door so that you can see who is entering when you are in bed. This will help you feel more at ease.

2. Make sure your bed is not in the direct line of the door. If it is, you will need to hang a crystal at the foot of the bed to disperse the chi. This will stop it from coming in through the door and quickly traveling up the bed, causing a physical imbalance

in your body and problems in your relationship. Also, make sure that you keep the door closed when you sleep.

3. Do not put your bed under a window, as that will affect the quality of your sleep. You need to place your headboard or the top edge of the bed frame firmly against the wall.

45

Enjoy Better Sleep and Better Sex with These 10 Essential Principles

As the place where you sleep and the place where you have sex, your bed is of the utmost importance. Here are ten essential principles for better sleep and better sex:

1. **King Beds:** Queen-size beds are better than king-size beds in the United States. That is because king beds are made up of two box springs, which creates a psychological split. If you already have a king-size bed, put a large red sheet between your box springs and mattress and imagine an improvement in your sex life.

2. **Drawers under Your Bed:** Do not store anything under your bed, as it creates subconscious blocks and hidden obstacles and can stifle your creativity. If you already have a bed that has storage drawers underneath, then store only items that are for sleep, like pajamas, blankets and sheets.

3. **Footboards:** Do not buy a bed that has a footboard that is higher than the mattress, as anything that rises above the foot of the bed can stifle your career.

4. **Headboards:** A headboard will give you a sense of stability and security. Make sure that it is strong and sturdy.

5. **Water Beds:** Avoid water beds as they do not create the feeling of stability necessary for a firm foundation in your life.

6. **Bedspreads:** Air should be able to circulate under the bed, so make sure that your bedspread does not touch the floor.

7. **Electric Blankets:** Do not sleep with an electric blanket, as it disturbs the body's natural electromagnetic system.

8. **Buying a New Bed:** The best times to buy a new bed are when you end a long relationship, move to a new home, recover from a major illness or are newly married.

9. **Wood vs. Metal:** Buy a wood bed, rather than metal, as wood is much more insulating and metal beds create a magnetic field around your body that interferes with healing.

10. **Futons:** Futons made of natural material like wood are great, but look for a frame that isn't too low, as it symbolically keeps your station in life low.

46 Attract a New Partner with These 7 Bedroom Changes

If you want to attract a new partner into your life, then try these seven simple actions:

1. Make sure that your bed is inviting and big enough for two. If you still own a twin or double bed, consider an upgrade to a queen-size bed.

2. Make sure that you have pillows and side tables on both sides of the bed, and matching lamps placed on each side table are a plus.

3. Make sure there is room for another person to get into the bed. Do not have one side of the bed up against the wall.

4. Clear out your closets and make space for a partner to hang their clothes.

5. Put fresh flowers in your bedroom to draw in new energy and change them regularly.

6. Take out any photos that represent old relationships or photos of you by yourself.

7. Put two stone statues together in the relationship area of the bedroom to draw in a stable relationship.

47 Cure Problems in Your Bedroom

Here are some of my personal favorite cures for the bedroom:

Bathroom in the Bedroom: If you have a bathroom in your bedroom, keep the bathroom door closed and the toilet seat down so that you don't let your relationship or health energy go down the drains in the bathroom. Put a mirror on the outside of the bathroom door, so long as it is not opposite the bed. Keep the air fresh and put a plant in the bathroom. (See tip #38 for other bathroom cures.)

Broken Doors: You must fix any doors that are not working properly in your bedroom. If you have one that is stuck, then you will experience some blockage in your career, so unstick it fast!

Ceiling Fans: A ceiling fan over the bed (desks and sofas also apply) can create physical and emotional imbalance, as the fan cuts through the chi. If you can remove the fan, then do so. If the fan cannot be removed, then hang a faceted crystal from the fan and keep it turned off. If the ceiling is extra high, you might not feel the effect, but I would not recommend having a fan on directly over you at night. If you must have it on, make sure that you are not directly under it!

Oddly Shaped Bedroom: If you have an oddly shaped bedroom, the best thing you can do is to make the room more symmetrical by adding mirrors to open up the space. Put a mirror on each wall that "encroaches" upon the space, which has the effect of pushing the walls out to make the room a rectangle. You can also hang a crystal from the middle of the ceiling to balance the energy out in the room (see tip #17).

Fireplace: If you have a fireplace in your bedroom, it can burn up the energy of your relationship, so I recommend that you don't use it. You may want to put a mirror above the fireplace to balance the energy in the room and some plants in front of it. (A quick note: Fireplaces can be a great or not so great feature in your home depending on where they are located. They are advantageous in the fame, family and knowledge areas of your home. If they are anywhere else, then you may want to cure them in the above way.)

48 Cure Slanted Ceilings

The best ceilings are flat and in proportion to the room that they are in. You don't want ceilings to be too high and you don't want them too low. However, many homes have slanted ceilings that are higher on one side than the other. In this case, the chi is forced down to whatever is under the lower part of the wall. If you have slanted ceilings in your office, then it is best that you reserve the area under the lower part of the ceiling for storage. If you have your desk under the low side, you may feel pressured or irritable at work. If you have a slanted ceiling in your bedroom, you don't want to put the head of your bed under the lower part of the ceiling, as it can give you troubled sleep and headaches and make you feel as if you are under pressure.

If you have no choice but to put your bed or desk under the lower part of a slanted ceiling, then consider using the following cures:

1. Hang a faceted crystal over the head of the bed or the desk to help dissipate any uneven chi.

2. Place a light that shines upward under the lower part of the ceiling and imagine it symbolically lifting up that side of the ceiling.

3. Place a plant that grows upward under the lower part of the ceiling to create an elevating effect and imagine it symbolically lifting up that side of the ceiling.

A ceiling that is slanted on both sides isn't such a bad thing, as the chi will flow evenly on both sides.

49 Cure Beams in Your Home

If your home has beams, it is especially important to be aware of where they are. A beam over your desk can block your career. One over your stove can affect your physical health and finances. If you have a beam over your bed, it can affect your marriage and your health. The beam over your bed is the one to really watch out for because if it runs above the center of the bed, it symbolically separates you from your partner and can have an adverse affect on the communication within your relationship. If it runs horizontally above a part of your body, it can affect your health and you may find that over time you develop a weakness in the particular area of your body that the beam is crossing. Consider the following cures for beams in your home:

1. You can paint the beam the same color as the ceiling, which has the effect of making it disappear into the ceiling.

2. You can hang a bamboo flute at both ends of the beam, at a forty-five-degree angle. This can create a very powerful lifting effect and is known to release any pressure that the beam is creating.

3. If the beam runs along a peaked ceiling, you can put two bamboo flutes on either side of the bed, on the wall at a forty-five-degree angle. If you don't want to hang flutes, then use an image of something that flies upward (such as butterflies or angels) so that the chi gets drawn in an upward direction.

50 Use Mirrors to Deal with Difficult Neighbors

You may have created the perfect feng shui in your home, but if you have difficult neighbors—if they are noisy or disturb you in any way—it can really affect the harmony in your home. Under these circumstances, place a small mirror in such a way that it faces your neighbors so that you symbolically reflect the problem back to them.

The mirror can be placed on the outside of the building, or it can be placed inside your home, behind a painting or in a cupboard, so long as it is facing in the direction of the disturbance. By doing this you are symbolically reflecting the problem back to the source and creating boundaries. You can even use a little compact mirror that you find in a pharmacy, or you can buy a special feng shui mirror online or in a store specifically geared to this purpose.

SO, HOW HAPPY *IS* YOUR HOME?

Now it's time to find out how happy your home really is—and how you can make it even happier. Take your quiz responses and follow the suggestions below to see which tips are best for you and your home.

1. **If you answered:**
   A. See tips: 3, 4, 21, 23, 24, 28, 29, 30, 33, 34, 36, 37, 41, 42, 43
   B. See tips: 3, 4, 21, 23, 24, 28, 29, 30, 33, 34, 36, 37, 41, 42, 43
   C. Congratulations on clearing your home of clutter. Now read on for additional tips to make your home even happier.

2. **If you answered:**
   A. See tips: 3, 4, 21, 23, 28, 40
   B. See tips: 3, 4, 21, 23, 28, 40
   C. Congratulations on fixing things when they need doing. Now read on for additional tips to make your home even happier.

3. **If you answered:**
   A. See tips: 1, 2, 3, 4, 15, 21, 22, 23, 26, 34, 37, 38, 39, 40
   B. See tips: 1, 2, 3, 4, 39, 43, 44, 45, 46, 47
   C. See tips: 1, 2, 3, 4, 25, 31, 33, 34, 38, 39, 40, 41, 43, 44, 45

4. **If you answered:**
   A. See tips: 1, 2, 3, 4, 15, 16, 17, 18, 21, 22, 23, 39, 43, 44, 45, 46, 47, 48
   B. See tips: 1, 2, 3, 4, 15, 16, 17, 18, 21, 22, 23, 39, 43, 44, 45, 46, 47, 48
   C. It's fantastic that you are happy with the relationship part of your life. Now read on for additional tips to make your home even happier.

5. **If you answered:**
   A. See tips: 1, 2, 3, 4, 38, 39
   B. See tips: 1, 2, 3, 4, 28, 38, 39
   C. See tips: 1, 2, 3, 4, 25, 38, 39

6. **If you answered:**
   A. See tips: 1, 2, 3, 4, 15, 16, 17, 18, 21, 22, 23, 24, 26, 34, 37, 38, 39, 48
   B. See tips: 1, 2, 3, 4, 21, 22, 23, 24, 26, 34, 35, 37, 38, 39, 40, 41, 48, 49
   C. It's wonderful that your financial situation has been improving since you moved into your home. Now read on for additional tips to make your home even happier.

7. **If you answered:**
   A. See tips: 1, 2, 3, 21, 22, 23, 24, 25
   B. See tips: 1, 2, 3, 21, 22, 23, 24, 25
   C. How lovely to walk into a warm and welcoming home. Now read on for additional tips to make your home even happier.

8. **If you answered:**
   A. See tips: 1, 2, 3, 4, 15, 17, 21, 22, 23, 24, 25, 29, 30, 34, 39, 46
   B. See tips: 1, 2, 3, 15, 17, 21, 22, 23, 24, 25, 29, 30, 34, 39, 46
   C. It's great that your social life has expanded. Now read on for additional tips to make your home even happier.

9. **If you answered:**
    A. See tips: 1, 27, 43, 44, 45, 46, 47, 48, 49
    B. See tips: 1, 25, 27, 43, 44, 45, 46, 47, 48, 49
    C. See tips: 1, 27, 28, 43, 44, 45, 46, 47, 48, 49

10. **If you answered:**
    A. See tips: 1, 2, 3, 25, 27, 31, 32, 33, 35, 37
    B. See tips: 1, 2, 3, 25, 27, 31, 32, 33, 35, 37
    C. Congratulations on having a great work setup. Now read on for additional tips to make your home even happier.

11. **If you answered:**
    A. See tips: 21, 22, 23, 24, 25, 27
    B. See tip: 25
    C. It's lucky that you see one of these rooms when you enter your home. Now read on for additional tips to make your home even happier.

12. **If you answered:**
    A. See tips: 1, 2, 3, 25, 27, 28, 33, 35, 43, 44, 45, 47, 48, 49
    B. See tips: 1, 2, 3, 25, 27, 28, 33, 35, 43, 44, 45, 47, 48, 49
    C. It's great that you sleep well in your bedroom. Now read on for additional tips to make your home even happier.

13. If you answered:

A. See tips: 21, 22, 23, 24

B. See tips: 21, 22, 23, 24

C. It's wonderful that you feel that your front door is really welcoming. Now read on for additional tips to make your home even happier.

14. If you answered:

A. These are great shapes for a home. Now read on for additional tips to make your home even happier.

B. See tips: 15, 16, 17, 18

C. See tip: 15

15. If you answered:

A. See tip: 26

B. See tip: 24

C. See tip: 26

16. If you answered:

A. See tips: 1, 2, 3, 4, 15, 21, 23, 24, 25, 28, 29, 30, 35, 36, 47, 48, 49

B. See tips: 1, 2, 3, 4, 15, 21, 23, 24, 25, 27, 28, 29, 30, 32, 35, 36, 47, 48, 49

C. How lovely to have such a harmonious household. Now read on for additional tips to make your home even happier.

17. **If you answered:**
    A. See tips: 1, 2, 3, 4, 15, 17, 21, 22, 23, 24, 28, 29, 30, 31, 32, 35, 37, 38, 39, 43, 44, 45, 47
    B. See tips: 1, 2, 3, 4, 15, 17, 19, 20, 21, 23, 24, 26, 28, 29, 31, 32, 35, 37, 38, 43, 44, 45, 47
    C. Congratulations on knowing how important it is to grow and evolve as a person. Now read on for additional tips to make your home even happier.

18. **If you answered:**
    A. See tips: 1, 2, 3, 4, 15, 16, 17, 18, 21, 22, 23, 24, 25, 26, 30, 34, 35, 37, 39, 43, 44, 48
    B. See tips: 1, 2, 3, 4, 15, 16, 17, 18, 21, 22, 23, 24, 25, 26, 30, 34, 35, 37, 39, 43, 44, 48
    C. How wonderful that your career has prospered since you moved into your home. Now read on for additional tips to make your home even happier.

19. **If you answered:**
    A. See tips: 1, 2, 3, 21, 22, 23, 24, 25, 27, 42, 50
    B. See tips: 1, 2, 3, 4, 19, 20, 21, 22, 23, 24, 42
    C. Congratulations on creating such a happy home. Now read on for additional tips to make your home even happier.

20. **If you answered:**
    A. See tip: 49
    B. See tip: 48
    C. See tip: 47

RECOMMENDED READING

Most of the tips in this book are based on the Western style of feng shui called the Black Hat School. If you want to read about it further, here are some books that explore the same style.

Feng Shui for Dummies by David Daniel Kennedy

Lillian Too's Basic Feng Shui by Lillian Too

The Western Guide to Feng Shui by Terah Kathryn Collins

The Modern Book of Feng Shui by Steven Post

Interior Design with Feng Shui by Sarah Rossbach

Feng Shui: Harmony by Design by Nancy SantoPietro and Lin Yun

Clear Your Clutter with Feng Shui by Karen Kingston

Fast Feng Shui by Stephanie Roberts

Sacred Space: Clearing and Enhancing the Energy of Your Home by Denise Linn

Feng Shui and Health: The Anatomy of a Home by Nancy SantoPietro

ACKNOWLEDGMENTS

Thank you to Mike Robinson and David Daniel Kennedy for bringing feng shui into my life at the times when I needed it most.

Thank you to my exceptional editor, Sarah Pelz, and the rest of the team at Harlequin for giving the *How Happy Is* book series a home. Tara Kelly, Mark Tang and Shara Alexander, thank you.

I would also like to express my gratitude to my fantastic literary agents, Shannon Marven and Lacy Lynch, for their hard work and unwavering support and to everyone at Dupree Miller. I would like to thank separately Jan Miller and Nicki Miser for being part of the team in the background. Thank you for pulling my book proposal out of the slush pile twice! It was obviously meant to be and proves that every now and again cold-calling can work!

Thanks are due to the *Huffington Post* and Scott Warren, Joel Mandel, Sam Fischer and P.J. Shapiro for bringing me to new pastures, and to Ashley Davis and Andrea Ross at CAA for being part of the team. Thanks to Laverne McKinnon for our inspirational hike and Eileen for giving me a home from home to write in.

Thanks also go to everyone at HowHappyIs.com, especially Jon Stout for his exceptional creative talent and Terri Carey for helping run the show.

Thanks to my parents, Richard and Susie, for such incredible support. To Nick for his unwavering encouragement and Phil for being such a stable force and a role model in so many ways.

To Stephen, Lindy and Hazel for welcoming me into your homes and giving so much.

Oli and Judah. My home. You rock!

Look for these other books in the *How Happy Is* series!

how happy is
your
Health?

50 Great Tips to Help You Live a Long, Happy and Healthy Life

Sophie Keller

**How Happy Is
Your Health?**

how happy is
your
Love Life?

50 Great Tips to Help You Attract and Keep Your Perfect Partner

Sophie Keller

**How Happy Is
Your Love Life?**

how happy is
your
Marriage?

xoxo

50 Great Tips to Make Your Relationship Last Forever

Sophie Keller

**How Happy Is
Your Marriage?**